# CRIES FROM THEIR CELLS

## When Walking On 'Forgiveness Road'

## By
## JANNETTE BARRETT

### Transitions Series: Book Three

**Cries From Their Cells: When Walking on Forgiveness Road**

Authored by Jannette Barrett

© Jannette Barrett 2021

Cover Images : Justina Justar Misdemeanor (author pic) and Shutter Stock
Internal Image belong to Jannette Barrett, Image of Audreia Josephs book cover
included with permission from Audreia Josephs and Mango Girl Publishing.
Edited by Marcia M Publishing House Editorial Team Published by Marcia M
Spence of Marcia M Publishing House, West Bromwich, West Midlands the
UNITED KINGDOM B71 1JB

**MARCIA M**
PUBLISHING HOUSE

# Dedication

This book is dedicated to myself and my fellow human beings, in the hope that they too can find their forgiveness road and walk safely upon it, removing their bitterness in order to step forward into the wholeness a free mindset can give.

# Acknowledging

The Almighty Creator
My husband, Paul
My Little sister.
Audreia Josephs
All my special community clients
My Church family.
The secure units.

# About the Author

My name is Jannette Barrett and I carry several Aka personas. My main two are: Ms Lyricist B and Machete. Besides being a multiple published author, I'm also an actor, singer songwriter, performer of poetry, a global narrator, a dance choreographer and Speaker. I'm married with three children and three grandchildren and have strong faith. I love to create, and be around like minded creative people who have a great sense of humour and free flowing spirits because I'm a generous humble giver who believes in the oneness of mankind.

# CRIES FROM THEIR CELLS

## When Walking On 'Forgiveness Road'

## By
# JANNETTE BARRETT

### Transitions Series: Book Three

# Prologue

When you care for another human being, whether in an intimate way or as an advocate such as a counsellor or mentor, a special bond is formed. Within that connection, an immense level of trust is built and, often, a deep sense of respect.

Writing my autobiography while caring for others has helped me care for myself; it's been an intriguing revelation. This final book of my autobiographical trilogy depicts how I've been finding out who Jannette Barrett really is, because I finally feel free enough to do so. The thing that intrigued me the most about myself was when I dared to step into the secure units to try and seek answers into my ex's behaviour towards me, whilst I analysed the men's conduct when they told me their stories. I'd already come to the conclusion that, in order for me to move forward with my life properly, I had to learn to forgive my ex, so listening and watching those men was valuable.

I have a woman by the name of Audreia Josephs to thank for getting me to a place of wanting to start the forgiveness process. She's my 'forgiveness guru.' Audreia has a wonderful way of shining the spotlight on what is damaging to you, and her approach helped me to open my mind enough to see beyond its capacity and focus on what I was praying for, which was wholeness.

Talking with the men, therefore, became a very educational experience indeed, not at all what I had braced myself for. After all that I'd been through with my ex, I expected to come away with some feelings of contempt, but I was using my senses accordingly and my mind was open, so I felt no judgement after hearing the 'Cries from their Cells.'

Nursing and caring have been my life's work since the age of two, because I was a young carer to my younger sibling. It was a lonely period in my life for at least a decade, even though I came from a large family household. The resentment I felt about being forced to bear the brunt of her care during my school years, because we were in the same year, began to dissipate when I realised the responsibilities of it were making me a more adaptable person. I can only guess that God gifted me with the type of mindset that could absorb the intricacies of care work but, at that young age, all I did was rebel and feel sorry for myself. Never once did I truly embrace the gifts I was blessed with.

When I finally accepted my inbuilt skills and ventured into the professional world of caring and nursing, predominantly on a one- to-one basis, I would never have believed that my bespoke approach, or 'bedside manner', would lead me to go behind prison bars and work as part of a team of professionals attempting to aid some of the inmates with their rehabilitation processes. I had already worked in some secure units - as well as nursing homes, hospitals and the community - but to work in a prison!

# Chapter One

## HEARING THEIR CRIES

*Can you put your hand up and say you always listen? Or have you been told."You never seem to listen, do you?" We can all be guilty of being overly consumed in ourselves in an unhealthy manner, I'm afraid, and so much so that sometimes a person can say to us, "Have you heard yourself lately?" This can be straight out of the blue and stop us in our tracks, thinking, "What the heck!" We can take it two ways: one, as an insult or, two, as a wake up call. I advise the latter. Listening works best if it's twofold. We must learn to listen to ourselves as much as we must endeavour to listen to others, and we must do so properly.*

The prison I was about to be involved with was the very same one I had been forced to enter many years prior, to see my abusive ex face to face, for the sake of our daughter. God really works in the most profound ways sometimes, so we really need to be mindful of what we pray for.

I was praying for wholeness. I prayed and I fasted so much and felt I was tested often, sometimes, way beyond my strengths. "God said He wouldn't let me endure more than I could bear" The Biblical verse of 1st Corinthians Ch 10. Verse 13 ends on: " He will not let you be tempted beyond what you could bear." New international version, but there are various versions to how this is stated. With this in mind, I thought I must soon see something but, no, there still wasn't anything made clear to me. Then, on feeling deeper emptiness from even more failures in those tests, It was obvious I would never find absolution without first learning how to find forgiveness, so I prayed and fasted for that to come as well as my wholeness, and this time I asked for it to come by any means.

First, I came across Audreia Josephs in a workshop. She happened to be a blast from my past when she and her family lived very close to me and my family way back in the early seventies. God was moving before me, setting up pathways for me to stumble onto without me even realising. He knew that if I so much as sniffed that I was being subtlety coerced into showing forgiveness to my ex, I would talk my way out of it somehow, delaying my wholeness, delaying becoming complete, which of course is what I was praying and fasting so earnestly for. God really does hear our prayers. I'm sure many of you reading now would be thinking, "Not me. I could never forgive a person, let alone an ex, that treated me like a bin liner; throwing nothing but rubbish my way, then discarding me. I get you, because I too was thinking that way."

The workshop consisted of all the techniques I was already using in my own line of working as a mental health freelance community practitioner. They were using art therapies, group scenarios, even theatrical performances. Wow! God placed me into a workshop where I was hearing the cries of women who had been hurt, and hurt like me.

The familiarity of what I was hearing made me feel as though I'd come into a circle of acceptance and love. The workshop was using all the skills that I wanted to revisit for such a long time, so not only did it tell me I was in the right place, but it told me that it was timely and it was where I would begin to learn how to forgive and move forward in my life, properly. What a great disguise God covered it with! He knew what I was thinking and He knew my heartfelt longing too. So He was answering my prayers and blessing them with an extra portion of my wants too, all by the grace of His love.

Amazing isn't even close to how I felt when I left that workshop, where I sat next to Audreia, who embraced me before confiding in me, telling me how she managed to overcome many painful things. I'd been doing that type of work with others all the time; helping them to adjust, focusing on all of their needs and their development by listening to their cries. But I failed to address my own wholeheartedly.

I read the email invite I received to go to the prison a dozen times while battling with various 'what ifs' scenarios. "What if, when I get there, I just can't go through with it? Will it look the same and make me panic? What about the smell? Will that trigger me?" My will was strong, so I fought hard to overcome my fears, as I knew there were already too many clues that led me to receive the email in the first place. And after the workshop, I knew It was indeed time for me to start the forgiveness process.

If I could do it, if I could go into that prison again, walk down those corridors, then talk with men that perhaps did exactly what my ex did to me or even worse, then walk out the other side, I'd be ready! Stepping into that prison would be the test of all tests, but I was determined to pass it, even if it would prove to be a huge challenge. I knew I had to do it: the need to be whole was too great.

I learnt how to love myself. I learnt how to forgive myself too with all my failures and shame. Yes, I did it and it was tough, but the triggers of my past still lay dormant, so I needed to forgive those who hurt me also, to finally put the past in its grave, unmarked and truly buried.

My daughter could always get me to do the impossible; she got me to face so much in the past. Back then, when I went to the prison to see my ex, her father, it was for her; this time it was for me and I had to do it by myself. Isn't it a strange thing how we can readily put ourselves in harm's way for our children but it's not that easy doing what's best for us if we think it might be dangerous or hurtful.

We are never cowards when it comes to our children. I would readily die for mine, but we can be pure yellow when it comes to ourselves. On that note, It gives me enormous pleasure to say, "Audreia Josephs, you would have been so proud if you saw me going down those corridors, with my head held high, walking on forgiveness road."

Before I was able to do this quite extraordinary act, however, care work gave me the much needed tools to carve my way through some of my clients' hard shells to discover the source of their vulnerabilities and speak openly and confidently to reassure them, "if I can, you can." I'd always say that, as we shared common ground.

All those years caring and nursing the ones who had mental health issues and addressing their every requirement inadvertently helped me with my most important development: the art of listening with a non-judgemental ear. Listening in such a manner assisted me with a stillness that penetrated the very fibres of my own mental health issues too. It was a valuable commodity to my wholeness, allowing me to adjust my thought processes, broaden my mindset and accept the flaws in myself as I accepted the flaws in them.

Inevitably then, when it came to entering the prison and speaking with the inmates, I found that my heart was empathetic towards them. I wanted to leave them with something tangible to hold on to by the time I left any session. I couldn't really believe how tolerant I was of them as they spoke. I am certain I got even more out of the sessions than they did, especially as I had some important theories and questions answered that had been plaguing my mind for so many years.

# Chapter Two

# BEYOND THE WALL

I have faced many walls in my life and I've felt that I would never get over them. Even running my many marathons, I've had blips where I've literally stopped and thought I'm just not going to make it, but I always did. I've never been physically behind a wall with a sentence hanging over me, looking at the wall every day, willing my mind to go beyond it. So I can imagine what was going on in the world I left behind, but my symbolic walls felt like Everest to me. It doesn't matter whether our wall is finance, a work situation, our relationships, communication with our children, or managing how we feel about ourselves. What matters is how it affects us and what lasting effects remain when we believe we have gone beyond our walls and came away from them triumphant. Triggers can still lay dormant, like sleeping bulbs in winter. So we must all take care to talk more, listen more, and because they can become fertile again and bloom, we must all be prepared to seek help.

I waited in my car for ages because I was far too early for my first prison session. As I approached it with its enormously high wall, even though I knew I wouldn't be in there too long, I already wanted to leave before I even entered. At the entrance, I could see that it looked as though I would be going in just at the same time as a change of shift. I was correct, because we all had to line up in the same line. I thought this was very strange, as I assumed the staff would be going straight in and definitely from a different entrance. I was wrong, of course, because we all had to be searched first.

I braced myself for the pending pat down, it was quite horrible, nothing like it is at the airport, probably because it was a prison with a totally different atmosphere and agenda than going on holiday. Once that was over, I was given a key to a locker where I had to put all my personal belongings. "Phew! I'm glad that's all over," I said to one of the guards. "It wasn't too bad." And the actual pat down wasn't too bad, except how it made me feel - and there was more to come. I had to endure yet another search, only this time it was by a sniffer dog. I heard, "Wait over there now, please, between those two lines for the dog handler." All I could think was that the dog would be a huge Alsatian, and it would sniff out my nerves then pounce on me.

What a relief it was to see, coming around the corner, a little pooch with his officer handler. My bag in the locker was bigger than that dog. A slight exaggeration, but it was a very small dog. It knew it's job though, and gave me a damn good sniff before moving to the next visitor. I then went through metal sliding doors with alarms, before gate after gate after gate, which all had to be opened with keys then locked behind after we had passed them and walked along corridors that were stark and cold looking. It was an eerie atmosphere, and not one I would want to work in at all. The enormous high wall was intimidating enough but now, all those gates, bars and corridors!

I just couldn't remember them making me feel so hopeless when I came before, maybe because, back then, I was full of hate and shame, and kept my head low so I saw nothing. Now! My goodness, what an awful claustrophobic feeling.

It didn't last long, thank goodness, as I was soon greeted by my contact who asked me how I was feeling. I didn't tell the exact truth. I held back a little and replied "Well, actually it's a lot more modern than I remember."

What I really wanted to say was that I was bricking it, but his presence made me feel so much better and I knew I would also have a representative from Mind, the mental health charity, with me too. Eventually, we arrived at the area where I would use all my senses and bring my magic touch.

The room wasn't very big at all, or was it that I felt so visible all of a sudden? I watched as, one by one, the inmates entered the room. They were all wearing their own individual clothing which was a relief for me to see, because they just looked like any ordinary bloke I would walk past in the street on a daily basis, even talk to. I watched as they chatted coming down the corridor, waiting for a particular section to be opened. They were certainly a lively bunch until they reached the room.

One by one, they looked me up and down in silence as they entered. Some smirked, others stroked their faces, and the rest walked in with a swagger clutching their crutches, staring me in the face as if I was their next booty call. That was a seriously uncomfortable moment, but I held my stance firm and didn't remove my glance from them either, even as I felt one bead of sweat drip down my back.

 "Don't you dare look scared Jannette Barrett; you got this."

My Lyricist B persona came to my rescue, as per usual, but I dismissed her and said internally "You're right, I've got this - *me*, so I'll do this alone."

# Chapter Three

# FIRST IMPRESSIONS, EMBRACED IMPERFECTIONS.

First impressions can be the reason we get a job or not, can't they? Don't you think they can be an unfair judgement though? If we don't look the part, it doesn't necessarily mean we cannot execute the job in hand. This, not looking the part, has happened to me so many times that I refuse to let myself fall into the trap of 'first impressions synopsis' with anyone else now. Falling into that trap can be costly to us and make us miss out on the right candidate, and that goes for labelling too. If we fail to embrace their imperfections, we fail to see the whole person, therefore fail to know if they were indeed suited. We are much more than what people perceive.

As it was my first session with them, I began with an exercise I've used many times before in my regular community safe space workshops. First, I introduced myself, which was often a shock to who was in the room, because I don't look my age or speak like they often imagine someone coming to counsel them would, and this was no different. 'I'm still baffled as to what I'm supposed to look like. Anyway, after I gave my short bio, I asked each of the inmates to also introduce themselves, just their name and how long they were in for, never what they did or didn't do.

Then I gave them my surprise; my golden nugget. All of their introductions were then mimicked by me. Their body language, tone of voice, even their accents and how they came across to me. It was received with both silence and smirks, before I said, "Did I get any of you right?" It was funny to hear the room fill up with comments such as, "You got Alan down to a tee," and "your Richard was a classic man, I swear". These two names, by the way, are fictional ones.

Now that the ice was broken and I could sense that they had a belief in me and were not at all put off. I began the deeper process of analysis.

I asked each one of them. "What do you want in life?" Then I asked them. "What don't you want in your life?" Then I asked them. "Do you want what you have?" I then asked them. "Now, can you be decisive?" Just those few questions opened their minds in a way that showed them I was more than willing to really listen to their stories individually, if they were willing to share them with me.

Each inmate displayed a longing in their answers, and that told me that each one felt remorse. I'm not a man, so, I can't think as one, but I could see their words in their body language to be sincere. Prison gave all of them time, and time allowed them to think. Prison took away their power, their choice, their independence and their identities somewhat. Without any of that 'clothing', they were all naked before me and I was able to see them for who they truly were: a bunch of men who made some bad choices based on reactions rather than responses. It got me thinking.

I knew that when I was angry with my ex, I would firstly want to shout out my argument, just to be louder than him and use words he probably couldn't understand. I would do this purposely, fuelling the argument and, if I was angry but was quietly handling it, I would clean and clean, taking out my anger on the furniture or kitchen cupboards. I chose my mood, not him. I chose how I would react and it was fuel with fuel, and it never ever made me feel better, only worse. On the other hand, he would instantly punch, kick or hit me with some object. Power was his choice.

He had to show more power than me, more dominance and, definitely, he needed to be in control. Was that a man thing? Or is that something a narcissist does, whether male or female? Is power one of the things that gets a man into trouble? Most definitely. But power used incorrectly can get anyone into trouble. My thoughts right now though are concentrated towards our menfolk. Is the thought of losing power and control the reason why they don't tend to talk about emotions, insecurities and their dreams? What about If they don't understand what they are feeling or there is a medical issue going on in their bodies! Could the reason they seize up be the lack of control they feel? The prison took away the control those men had. By me listening to them, it was a way to allow them a little of that control back, and it worked. I never know what to do if I don't feel in control of my situation, do you?

By the end of the session, which seemed to go very quickly, I was asked about my book. I had already told my contact that I was an author and a woman who had for a lifetime been subjected to various forms of abuse. So I wasn't just a qualified psychiatric nurse, but had lived experiences too. He must have told the inmates a little of who to expect and, from their interest in my book, it showed me they wanted a few answers too. Maybe, from my perspective also, they wanted answers as to why they may have treated their partners unfairly.

I only had the first one published at that stage, but had no hesitation replying, "Absolutely, of course you can have what I've got with me, " which was literally only three books. "I have written another book too but it's yet to be published; you can have a few of that one also when it's done." I was then asked to return, which I accepted, and I'm happy to report that I believe I've made great progress with some of those inmates, to the point that some of them have asked to pursue writing, add educational courses to help them bond with their kids when they are released. Others seemed calmer and were willing to tell others about going into the sessions.

I know that if it wasn't for the COVID pandemic, I would have been able to have reached many more inmates and given them much more of my time. Needless to say, I feel it's been a great start, and certainly an absolute pleasure on my part.

# Chapter Four

# I AM JANNETTE BARRETT

Have you ever questioned yourself with words such as. "Who the hell am I? Why have I allowed myself to put on all this weight? What on earth am I doing in this job? Where can I go from here? Why aren't I happy - I've got all I need?" Sometimes our lives are overly cluttered and we hang onto things that we really know, deep down do nothing for our self-esteem. Why I held onto so many size eight clothes in the hope I would get back into them was foolish when I'd crept to a size fourteen. All it did was make me feel fat. One size down is acceptable and manageable, not three. That's just one example in many. What I should have been holding onto was my passions in the hope of revisiting them. That's what keeps us alive, what drives us and prevents us getting swept away in a tide of stalemates where we forget who we are.

My name is Jannette Barrett. Damn, that feels good to say. I can't begin to express to you just how much, but I can at least attempt to try and tell you. I was finally free to be myself at the milestone age of fifty years old. At last, I could breathe an assured sigh of relief and look at the world with fresh eyes that were no longer hidden behind a mask. My future certainly seemed to feel very exciting indeed, and I really believed it could be, albeit there was now a considerable reduction in years ahead of me than years past. I was finally free to be myself! But I wasn't whole.

I wasn't moving forward in my dreams when I slept. My past was still a hindrance, haunting me, and I was still very much prone to triggers; that's why I had to begin to tell my truths by writing this autobiographical trilogy. I really believed that, after writing the first two books and having felt such a relief, the triggers would dissipate. I was free after all and finally myself, so why wouldn't they subside?

Just writing this section took me straight to those cells. When I first came through the gates and saw all the bars on the smallest of windows, knowing that someone was behind them, I wondered if they were feeling anything like I once was. Okay, I may not have been in prison like them, but I felt just as trapped. I felt that I hadn't had justice and I certainly didn't feel as though anyone was willing to see or hear me out.

Me not feeling free for such a long time - sometimes to the point of feeling suffocated, although I was able to do just about whatever pleased me - was most troubling. If it affected me to that degree, it must have been affecting those men all the more. They, presumably, questioned the judiciary decisions taken in their cases, thinking on whether they were given a fair sentence. Or how they perhaps felt when going for probationary measures but they weren't met because the powers that be didn't see what they wanted to see in them. I don't know; I can only guess their frustrations. I'm not saying I aimed to try and understand the depths of them; I merely wanted enough of an understanding to eliminate me from having a closed mindset.

To be heard, truly heard, can mean everything, because it's then that you are actually seen for who you are and where you are coming from. Everyone in life would aim to get a fair crack of the whip, wouldn't they? That's all I've ever wanted. Imagine studying for umpteen amounts of years so as to obtain a position in a certain career choice, only to be told you're not good enough because you failed the end of studies examination process, but you just knew you could do everything that was called for. What about being told you're too late, the positions are now filled up? Would you think you wasted your time, or would you continue to try again and again until you achieved what you set out to achieve? Willing to put yourself up for criticism, to be seen for who you are and what you studied for. That's my dyslexic life.

It took me a very long time to get to where I am, so there wasn't a chance I was about to waste any of the time I had left on this earth frivolously. But I didn't know what to do with the new-found self-release and belief I felt, and waited such a long time for. It felt monumental, like the greatest test of all, but I couldn't quite figure out why? It was okay for me to take my time on finding out, I thought, as it would be like an adventure. Those men, on the other hand, were subjected to rules, regulations and restrictions, institutionalising them. They may not know how to begin unraveling, especially if all they had ever been subjected to was challenging and their lives were simply an act of survival, like mine was.

I thought about them and whether they would be able to be true to who they really were internally, after having all the time to ponder on what life could have been like for them if they didn't follow certain traits or paths. We all have our 'what ifs?' moments. My work as a freelance mental health awareness practitioner was thriving as far as all my clients were concerned. To them, I couldn't put a foot wrong. Me! Jannette Barrett. "If anyone can, Jan can" is a quote often used regarding me, I'll have you know.

They actually speak highly of my character all the time; it's remarkable. And as for my personal home life, well, that's great too. I haven't even got an ounce of that empty nest syndrome some people get when their kids have fledged. Sorry kids, but I haven't; please don't take offence. I'm almost certain you all think, "Yeah, finally!" and are enjoying doing your own thing in your own way too, without me barking my orders at you, like my mother did with me.

Having none of my kids in the house hasn't changed my concepts, but it's changed my priorities, because they're all doing so well now. One thing I know they would all agree on is that I've learnt to listen to them more now, and have great advice to share. All that is thanks to my work. As hard as it is, sometimes the tasks involved in my work have helped me relax my mind enough to concentrate on my own needs at last, and I don't feel selfish to do it, either. That's a credit to my kids that I can explore myself and not be in the least bit worried about how they are all conducting their lives. Seeing their freeness is exhilarating to me, and I have to seriously pinch myself sometimes thinking I had a small part to play in making them excel.

There have been a few changes to the house, mind you, since they all fledged, like turning their bedrooms into a snug and an office. Oh yes, and there's something only my daughter and most women would appreciate. I no longer feel the need to wear my bra in the house, which is just heavenly. I can also leave the bathroom door open; in fact, every door is open at home now, and It's blooming fantastic. So how was it that I felt something wasn't quite settled within my core still? I was itching to find out what my other 'why' or 'whys' were, besides my kids and my husband. Where or what was my selfish happiness? I wasn't behind bars, but somehow I was also crying from my cell.

This career choice of mine has always shown me just how far I could stretch my patience and my endurance. Come to think of it, It seriously empowered my mindset for the greater good, I'm pleased to say. Another positive of doing care work was finding out just how long I could go without a proper cooked meal. Are you thinking, *I beg your pardon* ? Wait! Hear me out.

To begin with, the lack of having a good cooked meal was rather testing my mood. The many long hospital or nursing home shifts and the lack of sleep were intolerable most days. It was another reason I seemed to have been able to resonate with those inmates and listen properly to what they were saying. I'm sure meals of choice were not high up on the agenda, and sleeping through all the noise of the other inmates couldn't have been easy. Goodness me, with those two things combined, I could easily have turned into a grumpy old battleaxe of a woman, the kind of mood I can only assume many of the inmates had. Maybe I was a bit of a battleaxe to my kids at times, but I think it personally taught me how to be a better version of myself, and certainly more tolerant. That better version meant a better mindset. Still not buying it? Okay, I'll go further.

I began to think deeper, I questioned, "How can I maximise my full potential in this work environment?" See how my brain was turning that first resentment of caring towards my sister into a positive? "How can I help these clients feel better, which in turn would make me feel better?" In the end, I found I couldn't, unless I took control of my work situation myself, so I did. Taking control gave me back my choices, so I left the NHS conveyor belt care setting, because that never made me feel as though I'd finished caring for someone properly. Venturing out on my own to get back into the one-to-one care work I was practically weaned on was that missing piece after all. So there was my 'embrace'; the extra stimulus that gave me a positive mindset, and that's how I realised that, without real choice, how can we really be made fully responsible for what happens? Now are you with me?

Starting my Home help bespoke trade in 2004, Jan Can - which stands for 'Justified Assistance Necessary 4 Care and Nutrition - meant lots of cooking. It was a relief from being in the hospital or any nursing homes where clients only had a choice of perhaps two main dishes, or worse, taking what's offered. No! I wanted all my clients to have great nutrition, bespoke to their customised medical and cultural needs. It's amazing how much you change your own outlook on balanced nutritional cooking when you are considering someone else's health; it certainly made me aware of my own and got me questioning everything, from soil and water sources to where the foods came from, their duration, to packaging and what that packaging was made of.

I knew I had to introduce whole foods to stabilise the blood sugar levels in my diabetic clients, to help reduce their dependence on the medication metformin. For even the ones on insulin it was advantageous. On seeing their successful results, It was easy for me to begin eating a variety of whole and raw foods myself, along with full or intermittent fasting, which was proving better for my health, especially after my own two cancer scares. So again, there it was: caring for others allowed me to care for myself and venture into being the vegetarian I am today. My nutrition and exercise was at a healthy equilibrium, and my mindset was more stable. Oh yes, Jannette Barrett was proving to be quite rounded and I was on my way to my wholeness, but I hadn't realised that yet.

Clothes were the next huge change. Buying new clothes to help me feel better about myself was no longer necessary; not that the long nursing shifts left me with any strength to bother getting dressed up and going out anyway, much to my husband Paul's delight. Going out on the razz and straight into a night shift was no joke for him either, and actually very dangerous, as he's a driver.

Nope, all that went out the window the day I put on my first set of scrubs. Besides, I really love being at home, especially in our garden, playing music, having a barbecue when our kids come to visit or watching Netflix with my husband. I think it's been a very valuable lesson on evaluating merely what I wanted in life against what I knew I actually needed, and Paul felt pretty much the same thank goodness. Home life with our kids means everything.

So when this worldwide COVID-19 pandemic came, both of us were already equipped mentally to prioritise what was more important in our lives. Our safety, and our families financial stability, was the first priority, so a discussion on which one of us would continue to work had to take place. Of course checking on our children, as old as they are, was part of that process.

We knew we didn't want to both be mixing with all sorts of people in those early, uncertain days, just in case one of us got ill. We needed to make sure the other was able to be the head and conduct all the family's affairs. As I was in nursing as well as care work, and I still am, we thought it was best at that stage that I took the lead as the breadwinner; just for a short while, anyway.

This has been an interesting change in our relationship, because I found that I needed to put real time into listening to Paul and asking him how his day was. What usually took no time at all now took most of the evening, on and off, in between cooking or watching television. Again, I was able to tune into all I had learnt as a carer and what I had picked up by talking and listening with so many other men. It was strange, and felt different at home now we didn't have the kids to take our attention. With just the two of us, I was now using all the skills I'd ever used counselling at home, ensuring he was okay. It wasn't easy for him to take a back seat, especially when It turned out that we chose wisely, because his work load dried up to only half the amount, whereas mine doubled.

Writing had already proven to be my medicine, so I knew I wanted to continue in that vein, so as to have a balance. I didn't want my life to be all work and no play, but I still wanted more. Paul, thankfully, is an excellent all-rounder; he can fix just about anything, so had lots to occupy his mind in the home, in the garden, and working on his car. I was out there now, the real Jannette Barrett, and I quite liked her, so I thought about what else I would love to do.

I loved to dance, sing and act once upon a time, so could I now start all that again? Could I combine my chosen care and nursing work with art? Was that the selfish happiness I craved? Was that my cry from within and did I even have enough time in the day to add it in with all the extra workload? Of course I would have time, because when you know it's what's needed, you make it happen. Passion! That workshop with Audreia and going into the prison was all the proof I needed. I was born to care and use art therapies to make it bespoke. To me, It was God's will.

People were still asking questions about my first book, then after the second, it was more or less the same. "Why did you choose to write about your life? Will there be a third? Are you going to do anything else?" I was thinking, "Hold on a minute, give me a chance; I'm just getting to know who I am!" That's the essence, to the title of my second book. I would answer them of course in the best way I could and refer to my books as a backup reference if I got stuck. I did podcasts, interviews on radio shows, but still It didn't feel quite enough.

Then one day, that lightbulb moment came. All the in-depth information about me I'd just placed into peoples hands had provoked a reaction. The readers were now responding to this brave woman who triumphed against so many odds - like childhood sexual abuse, domestic violence, gaslighting, self-harm, suicide attempts, alcoholism and escaping prostitution by a hair's breadth - and was now a successful business woman in the field of care. They all seemed to want more of her - and so did I.

I guess I was feeling a bit scared to let myself die out, dwindle away and be in my opinion, nothing but an unknown again. I wanted to live up to Jannette Barrett with the formidable force that was loved and appreciated by many. The thought of returning to the persona I merely tolerated, wondering who the hell people were praising, was never again going to be an option. Talk about the worst case of imposter syndrome that I used to have riding through my veins like a sugar surge. I couldn't go back there again. No way! Not when I felt so alive with my new vibe.

Anyway, Jannette Barrett is my name and I have my crown firmly fixed upon my head. In fact, it's cemented on. To all my friends who have been calling me Jan, as I requested, I'm no longer going to say, "Just call me Jan" ,although I do prefer it. No, I am ready to own all of me; all Five feet two and a half inches of my short stumpy-legged, glorious self. Yes, I am ready to share with you all just how much I've fallen in love with me, and managed to combine art therapies with my job of assisting people.

I'll share more on how I learnt to forgive and even face narcissistic abusers, in the hope that I could shed some light on their distorted views of a relationship and give them a future with their children, despite their obvious family break-ups. I simply must share more of that, because I've seen the results already. Helping one has been a domino effect on so many lives for the better, and the children affected are always my priority. It's never a child's fault, in my view, and we were all children once, as were those men I met in prison. Where then did the faults lie in their or my ex's behaviours? What did the cries from their cells mean? What questions lay behind them and what answers did they all seek?

To assist me on that journey of self-discovery and total appreciation, I had to begin the very thing they all taught me. I listened. Oh, it is most definitely an art form. First, I learnt to listen more intentionally to the complimentary comments people said about me rather than merely brushing them aside, half-thinking that they were quite mad in their high opinions of me. Yes, I was finally taking those compliments on board. May I just throw this in the mix: If you have been brushing compliments off, as I have, just stopping that and replacing it with listening can change your whole outlook about yourself. It's so worth your time, and you are worth it, believe me.

It was my feelings of freedom, however, that enabled me to absorb them, so I'm not saying you will find it easy to do unless you have accepted all you are. But if you can manage it, at least try; it's a great self-confidence booster, and you'll be well on your way to self-acceptance. It proved so much so for me that, along with my whole name Jannette Barrett, I decided to use my Aka ('also known as), Ms. Lyricist B, too. If you've read my earlier two books to this trilogy, you'll know why I'm saying that was indeed a huge step up on my moving on in life.

That persona of mine has been a true companion in my darkest days. It's the only one that speaks fluently on all things positive and uplifting. It's the persona I use to write, sing and in most of my performances. Most importantly, it's the persona that never lets me down because, during my days of imposter syndrome, I felt I needed to keep my 'attack alert'. What's that, you may be thinking? Well, I wanted to keep myself sharpened.

When wearing the Imposter robe and mask, the pretence persona you have takes its toll on you. It's truly exhausting, so I would kickbox, run marathons, and jump from planes. I needed the adrenaline, the serotonin, the endorphins and a good dollop of dopamine just to keep myself feeling moderately happy and as fit as I could get. It was a true battle of wills.

When my husband came on the scene, he gave me all the physical love I could manage, but it was my spirit that needed consistency still, to bury some very dark demons.

The other reason for all the adrenaline stuff was to keep a worthwhile goal ahead of me, because I still felt so worthless. The more people commended me on those charitable achievements, the more I was able to hide behind the greatness of the task. Lyricist B, however, was always the one persona that kept me level-headed. I now enjoy all those adrenaline things for the fun element and not the distraction. I've changed. I've evolved. So, again, I ask you to think about what may be behind the partner you broke up with.

Did they have imposter syndrome? Were they playing out all what they were fed? Were they always fuelled by alcohol, drugs or both? Were they victims of abuse prior to meeting you? Men don't often reveal things like that; men don't even talk half the time. If you can get on that journey to forgiveness, primarily for yourself first, you may also find along the way that you learn to forgive them also and find the real you in the process. If not that, you will certainly be more broad-minded and tolerant.

This poem was written when I was drinking far too much and hiding behind humour.

## MENTAL HEALTH AND LONELINESS HAVE NO PARTIALITY

*I could be in a crowd or with my multitude of family, and say "I'm okay" but I had a hidden enemy. Mental health and loneliness has no partiality. Look at the celebrities, now that's the reality. They often have money like running water but that didn't alter the fact that they also succumbed and faltered. Mental illnesses are like the ripples from a pebble dropped in the river. They start tiny, but get wider and wider, spreading further and further then completely take over.*

*Our mental health and loneliness is something we hide and because we hide it we often collide with it. My PTSDs had me on my knees saying "forgive me please" to my family because the pills and booze that I had promised to lose when they asked me to choose, took me off the snooze button. That relaxed state of nothing, when my eyes rolled into the back of my head and all my troubles were shed, so I became rotten. I didn't want to face the forbidden. I wanted it to be forgotten. I knew without that snooze button I would panic, be hyperactive and erratic.*

*Oh the things I said when all was cleared and done, written upon their faces couldn't be undone. It made me want to run and run but I couldn't. Not one of us can get away from the contents of our own heads especially when we lay down in our beds , if we have one, No; not one. Yes I could be in a crowd or with my multitude of family and say "I'm okay." I can say that all day but I wasn't really. Trust me when I say it was a relief to speak the words, "I'm not at all okay" Truly. There's nothing scary about a reaction of silence; and sympathy won't kill. Not even a hint of negativity or ill will, no! What's scary is not being you, to be continually false and never true. Mental health and loneliness has no partiality generally, but maybe right now, it's particularly partial to you or was forever partial to your ex.*

That's food for thought, isn't it. Writing that was my cry out, and nobody saw it but me. It helped. It really helped. There are many foolish things done in a cry for help. I'm happy I have learnt to turn to writing as I have attempted suicide. Something I know men do more readily. That was a big part of me wanting to investigate how the minds of men think, and aim to forgive and try to understand them.

# Chapter Five

## A FEW PEOPLE THAT HELPED ME TO LISTEN

W*e can lose track of people so easily, like our school teachers or our university lecturers, because they are not people we link with when we are students. But what if we could? Would you thank them for what they did in your life? Perhaps not, because they were doing their job right! What if it was the other way around though. You've been helping people and they just get on in their lives and don't give you a second thought. Different now, isn't it? A little thank you would be appreciated. Sometimes it's good to look back for that very reason, and thank the people who helped us get to where we are. It's a healthy thing to do and gives us time to be grateful. Just give yourself a few minutes to think about who has helped you. It's a very worthy attitude to maintain your humility.*

Mr 1599

The thing about nursing and care work is that you have to adhere to some awkward shift patterns. There's some serious tiredness and lots of annoying noises. Most days I love the sound of the dawn chorus of birdsong. Sometimes, I think those birds purposefully lie in wait until they see me, and know just what I need, because they're like a welcomed ambush, or a beautiful birthday surprise. First they're peacefully perched in their various trees, sitting on the rooftops or balancing on lamp posts and then, as I put my key into my front door and lock it behind me ready to take my morning run in the fresh dew air, the tweet of amplified birdsong cracks the sweet silence of the night as if to release the sun from its slumber and give me a melody to run to.

"Good morning Lord. Thank you for this new day; I shall be glad for it." The days that start that way are when I feel at my best; when I feel so appreciative of life and all I have achieved. It's a sharp contrast to other days where I have to really concentrate on my temperament because things are the opposite way around and I'm coming home after a night shift listening to the noise of bowel sounds and snoring. I don't want to hear those birds then. All I can think of is, "Will they not even allow me to get in? Can I just take off my uniform, my shoes and run my bath? Flip me; I need a cup of tea and some silence."

My nights at work are full of strange noises. I know birdsong makes a beautiful sound really, but I truly don't need to hear them just as I get home. It's worse in winter as, any time I have left in a day, it's just too dark to enjoy doing anything. Summer, on the other hand, when the birds rise and sing at 3.30 a.m. to 4 a.m., even if I'm dog tired, I don't mind it at all, as  then the sun makes me happy, and being outside makes me happy.

When 6 a.m. arrives and I've finished a night shift, the birds are still chirping away like they've had a feast of fat worms and it doesn't bother me in the slightest. I'm ready to hand over my shift, go home, unwind and rest from the ringing monitor beep repeating in my ears amongst all the other muffled sounds I hear when nursing or caring for a client. I've had enough of that and I don't even want to hear them breathe; sounds harsh, I know, but the velocity of exhaustion I was feeling overwhelmed me. I just wanted to get outside and take in the beauty of what I see and how the sun makes me feel. Just imagine being locked up and seeing the sun and hearing the birdsong, but not being able to get out to experience it properly.

Another thing that's even more testing for me than the cold and the darkness of winter and a collection of annoying noises, is feeling tired. I mean the kind of tiredness I call 'delirium tiredness.'

Have you ever gotten to the point when your mind is still calculating but your body has dropped to second gear and you are aware that that second gear isn't good? That happens to me when I've used so much adrenaline driving my body that I've gone into some kind of lactic acid overload, it ain't much fun being there. I think anyone in the healthcare industry finds themselves there quite regularly, whether a doctor, nurse, health care assistant or paramedic after a double, back-to-back shifts of twelve or fourteen hours.

Oh the screaming limbs, the dry eyes that are shut from seeing anything, even though they are forcibly wide open, and that unrecognizable mumbo jumbo language coming out of your mouth like you've had four double whiskeys without a chaser. Twelve or fourteen hours of hard work I'm moaning, but I'm not in a cell. I'm screaming inside, but I can still go outside when the shift is done.

I am a freelancer so, sometimes, not much nursing is required in my work, but a great deal of care is, and that comes with plenty of dialogue. I'm fairly adaptable and can confidently care for clients that have mental, physical, drug or alcohol dependence, learning or even sensory impairments. With this wide range, I'm often called to help out a family with what is referred to as 'respite care', so that they can go on a well- deserved, battery-recharging holiday. This is when I have to 'live in'.

Now, I always try to put my feet into the shoes of the person I'm about to care for as soon as I can after an initial risk assessment. I do this to create some common ground in order to get some comfortable compromises in situ. It's never ever a totally smooth transition when you are in their home, so It always helps to imagine they may be feeling rather put out when watching their family go off on holiday, and perhaps almost a burden. I recognise the signs of that feeling very well, having looked after my own autistic little sister throughout our school years, as well as care for my mother during her cancer and my father after a stroke. So, I thought, it would be nice if I made them feel like they were on holiday too, getting their own, fully bespoke, one-to-one all-inclusive.

I'd begin to find out what they enjoyed doing, where they liked to go, that type of thing, which often included swimming or walks in the park, and feeding the ducks, or going to the cinema and bowling, all of which can take quite a lot of energy on my part. I do it to keep their minds actively functioning, positively, with a daily purpose in mind. I thought it was paramount, especially if they happen to have a dependence on a substance.

Did you just clock what I wrote there? Me and my old imposter syndrome self was checking on this with clients, and I never did that with myself. "To keep their minds actively functioning, positively, with a daily purpose in mind." Well, blow me down with a feather! I knew then that that was paramount. Even in the depths of my sorry, self-pitying state, I knew how important it was to have a positive outlook in your life. No wonder they thought highly of me. No wonder I could resonate with those inmates and them with me. That old saying comes to mind. "It takes one to know one." Now, back to the story; I just needed to make sure you digested that bit,because it's huge. Bragging over.

Right! After a series of very trying days and nights living in, doing all manner of care chores and excursions, it would start to catch up on me. I'm no superwoman. Imagine resting your eyes because you really have to, but you shouldn't. They're so dry, and burning to close, that you simply must obey them. Then something creeps up on you: a complete, involuntary set of visions (hallucinations), or the delirium tiredness I spoke of earlier sets in, where you have confidently believed you have gone to assist the client with some basic but necessary care. It could be something like draining their catheter bag, turning them to relieve pressure, but ever so gently, so as not to fully wake them, then going to the kitchen to make yourself a cup of tea - but none of it actually took place at all. You realise you are in fact still sitting on the chair close to their room listening to the monitors and the other night sounds. Moments like that reminded me of my heavy drinking days and the thoughts I carried. It reminded me yet again of those inmates and the cries from their cells. It's unbelievably weird how your minds can travel from place to place in your memory library.

Life as a carer can be very difficult but also very rewarding, but who would choose it as a career? The pay is absolute rubbish, if it's not privately paid. The hours are staggered and long, and it's domiciliary! Come on, that's really pants, but I love it, including caring for all sorts of people that started at home with my little sister. Yes it made me who I am today, and I think I'm pretty awesome now.

It's taught me a multitude of things that have built my character, like patience, endurance, gratitude, humility. It's also taught me the art of listening, my most powerful tool, and that's only mentioning a few. How patient do you think you are? Doing care work makes you develop the patience of an expectant father waiting for his wife to give birth to their first child and not falling asleep. Not falling asleep! Oh yes, stop babbling Jannette. Back to the tiredness. That's the big drawback of this career, and none is worse than when you have to also be quiet, but stimulation is what you need. I could do with the dawn chorus of birds then. I've really had some phenomenal clients, and some will remain in my heart forever like Mr 1599.

Mr 1599, or Mr E. Of course, that's not the real number of his house or anything, but there's no way I'm giving his name away, because of patient confidentiality and all that. Besides, I have the utmost respect for him, even now. What a character. He was an engineer and pilot in the Royal Air Force and flew a Lancaster bomber but hated flying. Go figure. Anyway, I was asked by a wonderful woman, I will shed more light on later to tend to Mr E. It was only with some basic pastoral care; nothing tasking. That's another care term you may or may not have heard of. It's basically care that tends to a person's social need, aiding their mental wellness.

He unfortunately lost his wife a little over a year prior, and they were besotted with each other. Mr E actually cared for his wife himself during most of her illness and was still driving her to her hospital appointments when he was in his very late 80s. He was incredibly devoted. On hearing all this about him, I was moved as well as honoured to try to assist him. Now I have dyslexia, oh wide-eye alert! Yes, it's taken my publisher time to get used to my way of wording, and you are doing just great reading it, aren't you? Well, Mr E was very intellectual, and spotted my back-to-front phrasing of things instantly.

Now he could have made me feel rather inadequate but, no, he just listened, then politely corrected me by rephrasing my sentencing. "Did you mean to say, would I prefer to have porridge rather than marmalade on toast this morning?" This was after I said "Am I getting you some marmalade toast with porridge?" I think this was good for him, playing teacher-student with me. Touché. it gave him purpose and he felt that he was doing me a great service. He was teaching me how to listen and respond correctly and patiently.

We clicked quite quickly, because he had a brilliant sense of humour too. I'm not sure what it was about me that he liked, as we couldn't have been more worlds apart. I could really get my male clients to open up and talk freely, and even ask me to be an advocate for them. They were tools that came in handy in all aspects of my career and life.

Judy Dyke MBE was the woman that referred me to the family of Mr E. We became true friends, Judy and I, after I helped her care for three members of her own family. She always had time to listen to me, and her advice to this day has always proved valuable. Judy went on to write a foreword in the second book to this trilogy, called "I don't know who I am." Mr E and his wife didn't have children, but did have two nieces, but they lived too far for regular visitation, so that's where I came in. Mr E actually helped many others gain caring skills due to his needs, extending to 24 hours of a full care package, so I had to get a team in to assist me.

Working with a team on his behalf showed me even more ways of handling various temperaments, and at the heart of it, there he sat, listening, advising and sometimes barking orders. He was a very fair man, who was disciplined and conscious of everyone else's needs.

The tribute I gave at his funeral was very fitting, and I'll never forget what he contributed to all of us in the team.

Mr K

Oh Mr K. What a gentle heart. Him and his little dog were an absolute delight. He was never any trouble to care for, and he was always up for a cup of tea and a natter; another great listener. He once told me some of the upsets in his marriage and where he thought he could have handled things much better but, in those days, the man was considered the breadwinner and the wife kept the home.

On hearing some of his issues involving disagreements, I could see his remorse instantly, and he was almost physically kicking himself at his stubbornness to back down. It was never expected that a man backed down from a decision, especially in front of a woman, wife or no wife. I asked him at that point if he thought men's behaviours had changed since then. His reply was, "Only the gay ones might have backed down." There were a few things in what he said about his past that I knew I would have found difficult to tolerate, yet at that moment, there was only the kindest and gentlest man speaking to me.

Mr K was a successful business man before retirement and had two sons. I figured that he must have had to handle many disputes over the years. So, it was interesting to hear his views on a man's dominion. Again It got me thinking, if I had more brothers not just the one, if I had seen how they behaved and learnt how to understand them, would I have been subjected to an abusive relationship? All this listening, all this seeing things from a male perspective was really opening my eyes.

# Chapter Six

## OPENING UP

TRUST. *These days, it's not easy to trust others. The world seems so corrupt and there are so many scammers polluting our thinking. What if I said to you, "Just trust yourself and trust will then start to come with other encounters." I'm speaking of GUT INSTINCTS. They are our safest bet. Trust has to be earned; isn't that what people say? If that's the case, can't we also regain it if it comes from a succession of events?*

Opening up has got to be one of the hardest things to do. So many of us don't own up to how we really see or feel about things. We've grown accustomed to allowing ourselves to be manipulated into the status quo; into a conformity that we often don't agree with but go along with because it's less confrontational to just fit in and live a quiet life. This is a dangerous road, as it drains our trueness to the point that we become a stereotype.

My second husband took me on with two children in tow and he has been the king of listeners. If he wasn't like that, I wouldn't have trusted myself to open up to him like I did, even if I had the hots for him like crazy. I had everything bad about my life wound up so tight, that when I started to unravel to him I was like one of those old cassette tapes. I kept getting stuck and didn't know what to do or how to react with him because I was plagued with my awful memories, but Paul just listened patiently. It didn't matter how many times I paused, rewound or jumped forward,  he was ready to pick up all the loose 'tape' that I unravelled, wind it back up and play the cassette back to me. That's how I knew he had listened to every single word I said. Yes, my husband listened to my cries from the cell and he helped me to heal, but it took years.

I don't know why so many men find it difficult to talk about their feelings. I don't know why they find it difficult to show them, either. What I do know, however, is that they do want to talk, but most of them just don't know how. They fear criticism more than us women, and that's probably because us women criticise ourselves every day. It's commonplace for us; we literally are doing our best to unlearn that. I've never known a decade like the one just past where almost every female platform, group or message has something to do with self-love.

The macho male image has so much to answer for. It's a killer of men. If a man falls into that false perception that they must look, act and talk a certain way to a woman, be 'all man' or they won't appear attractive to us, then they have already lost us. I certainly was never attracted to any form of male Chauvinism, and I don't believe many other women are either. What we want is a man that hears us, sees us, understands us, communicates with us and, above all that, loves us unconditionally. So if that's what we want, isn't it logical that a man may also want all those qualities in a woman to be given to him?

How often have we sat with our partners and given them the space to speak openly about how they feel without us interrupting? I've chosen to use the term partner as not all of us are married, and some of us are in same-sex relationships. Well, have you done that? Or is it more like this scenario: "Hey babe, how was your day? Gosh, mine was absolutely awesome. I had this woman, right, she was saying how great I was at hitting my target and ...". Your partner didn't even get a second to answer.. If that's done often, then he just ain't going to open up any time soon now, is he?

Our enthusiasm can be so selfish, and we just don't see it because we are full to the brim with us; there's no room to fit anyone else in. A man can sometimes feel we've got too much to say and, by the time he has given his time to try and listen to us, he doesn't even want to begin to talk about what he's been up to. And what about the fact that society tends to lean towards the man providing the best Valentine's Day, and Mother's Day? Is that even fair? I'm not overly fussed, but some women will argue if they didn't get what they want, or their partners forgot entirely.

My point is this: if our partners can get into the flow of talking to us, knowing we will actually listen, not criticise, then they may begin to feel more relaxed about talking amongst themselves and to their doctors or, if necessary, seek counsel, and many more relationships could be saved.

**Some of My Tips**

What I'm sharing here came with a firm kick up the rear - I'll kid you not. They're the best tips I've ever received, that's why I still use them.

1.Don't argue.
Ha! Seriously, it just doesn't work. Both parties are adamant that they are in the right and it will drag out until one backs down. That person then feels that you didn't listen and don't respect their views. Remember me saying that a woman wants to be heard and seen and the same goes for a man? So what do we do? We listen with a non-judgmental ear. Yes, you can do it! Keep your voice calm and simply say, "Okay, you go first." Then just listen. Believe me, even if you think they are wrong, the fact you gave them space to talk, will make them feel better and much more respected. Once that process gets digested, they are more responsive and may listen to your view. You could, but not always, reach a comfortable compromise.

2. Admit your wrongs (in its weight.)
Wrongdoing is a virus in a relationship. Sometimes, saying sorry ain't enough: you have to show how sorry you are to the value of the wrongdoing. It's the same as saying I love you. If you don't show it, it's just words, and those three words can seem empty and emotionless. The best time to admit your wrong is the minute you realise you've made that mistake or the minute you've

been found out. Don't drag it out or make excuses. Show your remorse and demonstrate your regret.

3:-Let it go.

Oh dear! I know that some of us can hold onto a grudge like it was a prized possession. It's possessive, certainly, and not at all healthy. Some of us hold on to it as a 'what if weapon' : If he so much as starts that crap, I'm going to tell him, "Remember when you did..." . No, no, no. Let it go!

Everything I've just listed boils down to listening. Active listening. Sometimes we think we have listened but, if we were asked questions, most of us will only be able to answer half, possibly a third, of questions about the conversation we were listening to.

Listening to those men in prison has given me a deeper understanding and a broader mindset. I've said that, but I haven't said why. Well, my reason was a selfish one to begin with, that I'll admit, because we are dealing with truths here. I was already prepared to listen, because I wanted to be released from my past and be able to find forgiveness from my heart so I could move on with my life. In my seeking, I got a lot more than the release after hearing the cries from their cells. Not only did I find the room in my heart to forgive my ex, but the love for myself, my husband, children, siblings, fellow man all increased because my heart no longer contained any hatred. Now that's what I call a result, considering it came from what I continually said I would never, ever do.

# Chapter Seven

## BEYOND ME

Your opinions are yours and we live in a *democratic society, so you are more than entitled to express them. It is wise, however, to also value the opinions of others, even if we do not always agree with them. I say this because we are constantly evolving, and those very opinions first dismissed are often ones that we value and appreciate later. Have you found yourself remembering an opinion you first rejected as foolish but now consider it valid? Seek the bigger picture, the wider viewpoint, the fuller meaning, the broader perspective, and you may find yourself a much more tolerant and approachable human being.*

I am but one woman, but I feel it in my bones that, collectively, if all us women, all of us who have begun the journey of self-love, self-empowerment, self-renewal and projection through all the channels of health and wellness. If we begin to just listen, really listen in the same way that we ourselves want to be heard. Oh my word will our King's shine.

How wonderful will our young princes bloom? How much more articulate will they stand and speak when they know they will be heard? How much more engaged with us will they be? How much more will we learn if we exercise a non-judgmental ear?

I'm doing what I can. I'm developing because I am now listening. I was prepared to go where I was afraid to go in order to ensure I moved on in my life properly. I was prepared to let go. It's almost indigestible to me that I have finally, after thirty years, learnt to forgive my ex, who damaged me in such a way that I couldn't find myself, even after having my children and marrying the man of my dreams.

Marriage and children cannot fix you if you don't know who you are or if you hold regrets and hatred in your heart. How can you fix something when you don't know what or the parts are? It would be like having a flat pack without instructions. Worst still, not having any means like glue, nails and a hammer to put it together. We must all remove these obstacles that prevent us from growing into the true, kind, spirited beings we are. We must give ourselves a clean slate to work from; a nice, blank canvas to paint on when building a relationship and family. Yes it can prove tough, but it's worth it, and you are worth it. I was like broken glass. My fragments were all over the place. I was like the Christmas tinsel you find six months later, after umpteen sessions of vacuuming.

Time was the pan and brush that swept up my fragments. Faith was my glue. But it was my husband and all those clients that taught me how to listen that stuck me together again after I was firstly willing to listen to myself. Then all the above, with God's grace at the helm, delivered me into the hands of Audreia. That led me into the prison; the same prison where I sat listening to the lies from my ex all those years before. Now I listened to men and the cries from their cells then, finally, all of it allowed me to move on.

MY LEGACY

My autobiographical trilogy is now part of my legacy. I hope I will be remembered for my honesty, my passion to give bespoke care, my unequivocal drive to pursue wholeness, and my devotion to love and be there for my family.

The cries of a woman can be seen and heard - that's one thing we do very well. The cries from a man are often silent, but it's theirs that scream the loudest. Please talk to one another. Please give time to listen intently and properly. Please be aware of silences and, most of all, stop lying to yourself.

# Epilogue

Writing my autobiographical trilogy has been one of the toughest things in my life to face, but it has also undoubtedly been my biggest single-handed triumph. My children are obviously my joint biggest triumphs, and I couldn't be more proud of each of them.

I call myself "A Proud Dyslexic" but, right now as I write this, I'm thinking of stretching that to "Super-Proud". I began my memoirs in 2018 with book one and, each year, I've developed from where I was. In 2019 came book two, and in 2020 I wrote, directed, produced and starred in my own play based on my memoirs in books one and two.

Now you have just read the third and final part, and it's this book that I'm actually the most proud of, and it's not because it's the completion. It's because I've seen just how far I have come and I've conquered the most challenging thing: Forgiveness of my ex and the uncle that abused me from the age of three. That's huge.

I ended part two of book two entitled *"I'm finally free to be me!"*

I'll end this book with this: ***I'm finally whole.***

# References

**Ms. Lyricist 'B' Author and poet**
@134RCB21

ART IS WORK🎤🎙️🎬✍️

Mrs Judy Dyke M.B.E #Tyndallwoods Solicitors

**Life Community
Church**
Religious
organisation

https://www.amazon.co.uk/dp/1530067669

www.marciampublishinghouse.com

Printed in Great Britain
by Amazon